C.C. and the Alamo Cats

bright sky press

2365 Rice Blvd., Suite 202 Houston, Texas 77005

Copyright © 2011 Daughters of the Republic of Texas.

No part of this book may be reproduced in any form or by any electronic or mechanical means, including information storage and retrieval devices or systems, without prior written permission from the publisher, except that brief passages may be quoted for reviews.

ISBN 978-0-9819904-2-2

10 9 8 7 6 5 4 3 2 1

Library of Congress Cataloging-in Publication Data on file with publisher.

Art Direction and Design by Ellen Peeples Cregan
Illustrations by Don Collins
Printed in Canada

C.C. and the Alamo Cats

William R. Chemerka
Illustrations by
Don Collins

bright sky press
HOUSTON, TEXAS

*This book is dedicated to
the Daughters of the Republic of Texas
who have cared for the Alamo, the Shrine of Texas Liberty,
and its cats
for over 100 years.*

Acknowledgments

Thanks to the following cat lovers who helped make this book possible: Mary Jo Mastrangelo, Pattie Sandoval, Charles R. (Rusty) Gámez, Caitlin Donnelly, Leslie Sitz Stapleton, Chuck Tucker, Rachel Dominguez, Sally Koch, Juan Gusman, Tawnny Mohn, Dr. Bruce Winders, Debbie Chemerka, Audrey Tyler, Rita Kerr, the staff at Bright Sky Press and the Daughters of the Republic of Texas.

Introduction

The story of *C.C. and the Alamo Cats* began long ago, even before the famous Siege and Battle of the Alamo in 1836.

Cats probably roamed the grounds of the Alamo when it was a Spanish mission in the 1700s, and they possibly lived among the ruins of the mission in the early 1800s. Some say that a cat was inside the Alamo in 1836 while the defenders waited for General Santa Anna's soldiers to attack.

Over the years, tall tales and legends have been told about the Alamo cats. This book tells the stories of such legendary cats as Skeeter, Tooz, Wuckie, Red and Tuxedo. And readers will also learn about Ruby, a loveable cat who lived at the Alamo in the 1980s. Of course, C.C., the most famous of all the Alamo cats, is featured here, too.

The story of the Alamo is, however, more than just cats. The Daughters of the Republic of Texas, who serve as the official custodians of the Shrine of Texas Liberty in San Antonio, Texas, welcome everyone to visit the Alamo and learn more about Texas' historic fight for freedom and independence.

Remember the Alamo!

Skeeter
1846

TEXAS RANGER BOB WAS GLAD TO RETURN to San Antonio. It was the home of the Alamo, the place where the famous battle for Texas freedom had been fought ten years earlier.

He arrived at dusk and dismounted. He patted his dusty trousers and wiped his face with his blue-checked bandana. Ranger Bob removed his large-brimmed, black hat and placed his right hand over his heart. It was his way of honoring the Alamo heroes.

Ranger Bob appreciated the quiet and peaceful atmosphere at the old mission.

Suddenly, he heard a mosquito buzzing around his ear.

"Pesky skeeters," he mumbled as he swatted the insect away with his hat.

Then he heard another sound.

"Meow."

He looked around but saw nothing. Then he heard another "meow."

Near the corner of the Alamo Church, the old Spanish mission building which protected the women and children during the Alamo siege in 1836, a fluffy gray and white cat suddenly appeared and jumped after a bug.

"Get that skeeter!" cheered the ranger as the cat leaped at another insect flying by. The cat knocked the mosquito to the dirt and played with his tiny trophy for a few moments. His left paw partially covered the insect until the winged creature started to fly away. But in an instant, the cat's right paw knocked the mosquito to the ground.

Ranger Bob was amused by the cat's antics. He approached the cat slowly and bent over to pet him. The cat purred and rubbed against his dirty boots.

"You remind me of a cat I had when I was a little boy," he said. "You sure do. He was a real friendly critter, just like you."

"Meow!"

"I bet you're hungry," said Ranger Bob. "Catching bugs is hard work, even for a little lion like you. Let's see what I can fetch for you."

The cat looked up at him and meowed again.

Ranger Bob reached in one of his saddle bags, pulled out a small piece of dried beef and placed it on the ground in front of the cat. The cat sniffed at the offering and quickly ate the scrap of meat.

"Slow down now, you Skeeter," he chuckled. "That's it: Skeeter! That's what I'm calling you from now on." The cat looked at him again, hoping for another piece of the beef.

"That's all I have left, Skeeter," smiled the ranger. He gently petted the cat and Skeeter purred with every gentle stroke. After a few minutes, Skeeter curled up and went to sleep at his feet. The cat looked like a big ball of gray and white fur.

Ranger Bob smiled as the cat twitched his whiskers as he slept. Every now and then his long tail would swish back and forth.

"You must be dreaming about catching more bugs," he said quietly. "So I sure don't want to wake you up."

The ranger mounted his horse and glanced back at the cat. "I've got to leave town for a while, but I'll be back," he said. "You keep defending the Alamo from all those skeeter bugs."

As the ranger rode away, Skeeter awoke. The cat briefly looked at the departing ranger and curled up again. Within minutes, Skeeter was dreaming again.

Texas Ranger Bob didn't return to San Antonio for several months. While he was away, the ranger tracked down outlaws and helped ranchers locate their runaway livestock. When he came back to San Antonio he paid his respects to the Alamo heroes and looked for the cat.

"Skeeter!" he said in a soft tone. "Where are you? I've got something for you."

He spoke louder: "Skeeter!"

Ranger Bob looked toward the back of the Alamo Church but saw no sign of the cat. Then he looked toward the abandoned Long Barrack building. Skeeter was nowhere to be seen.

"Well, I guess you've found another home," said the disappointed ranger. "I'll sure miss you, though."

But two tiny ears soon rose up from behind a chunk of limestone near the Long Barrack building.

"Meow."

"Howdy, Skeeter," he said with a large smile. "For a moment, I thought you might have moved to a new home."

The ranger dismounted and opened up his saddle bags. "Have I got something for you!"

Texas Ranger Bob placed pieces of dried fish on the rock. Skeeter scampered over and ate all the fish. When he was finished he licked his paws and rubbed them against his furry face. He looked up at the ranger and delivered a contented meow.

"I knew you'd like that," said the ranger.

After the cat finished eating, Ranger Bob petted Skeeter. The cat started to purr, but it quickly darted back inside the Alamo when a wagon pulled by a team of horses rumbled nearby.

"It's only horses, Skeeter," he said. "Don't be afraid."

Skeeter ran behind an old wooden barrel; he felt safe there. He curled up and started grooming himself. Then the sound of birds got his attention. He quickly abandoned his location and quickly ran after the low-flying flock, but the birds landed safely on top of the Alamo Church.

Ranger Bob was impressed by Skeeter's energy and playfulness.

"You are a lively little critter, that's for sure," he said. "Now be good until I see you again. I'm going to get a room in town for the night, but I'll be back tomorrow."

Skeeter turned his bright yellow-green eyes at the ranger and went right back to stalking the birds.

"Adios, Skeeter," said the lawman as he rode away.

The next morning Ranger Bob was back at the Alamo with more scraps of beef for the cat. As soon as he rode up, Skeeter appeared.

"I sure hoped you'd be around, little fellow," he said as he placed the meat on a small stone. "I know you'll enjoy this. Eat up!"

When Skeeter finished his food, he cleaned himself and walked over to Ranger Bob.

"I know what you want now," said the ranger as he rubbed Skeeter's back. Ranger Bob spent the rest of the afternoon with the cat because he knew that his next assignment would keep him away from the San Antonio area for quite a long time.

Texas Ranger Bob had been assigned to patrol another area in East Texas beyond the San Jacinto River. He was going to be responsible for tracking down cattle rustlers and horse thieves.

While he was on duty, Texas Ranger Bob would think about Skeeter. He made a promise to himself that once he completed his patrol he would return to San Antonio and find the cat.

But a war broke out between the United States and Mexico in 1846. Bob and others rangers served as scouts for U. S. Cavalry units stationed near the Rio Grande River.

The fighting raged for a few years until U. S. military forces captured Mexico City. As a result of the treaty which ended the war, the United States won a large tract of land that extended from Texas to the Pacific Ocean. Eventually, several new states were created from the land. In Texas, the Alamo became a military post for the U. S. Army.

Ranger Bob finally returned to San Antonio during the winter of 1848. It had been over a year since he had seen the Alamo and Skeeter. It was a particularly cold and wet January day when he arrived in town and the daytime rain turned to patches of ice. He was very concerned about Skeeter.

"Skeeter! Skeeter!" he shouted. "Where are you?"

It was very quiet.

Ranger Bob didn't see the cat near the Alamo Church or the Long Barrack building so he slowly rode around the old mission. But Skeeter was nowhere to be seen. He got off his horse and walked around the buildings which were now occupied by U.S. Army soldiers.

A sentry approached him.

"Halt!" stated the sentry.

Ranger Bob paused.

"You have business here, sir?" asked the sentry.

"Yes, you might say that," replied Ranger Bob. "I'm from the Corps of Rangers."

"I don't see a badge," questioned the sentry.

"We don't have official badges, but I have this document which grants me the authority to uphold the law," said Ranger Bob as he handed the official paper to the sentry.

The sentry read the document and handed it back to Ranger Bob.

"So, how can I help you?" asked the sentry.

"Believe it or not, but I'm looking for a cat that used to live here," said Ranger Bob.

"A cat?" questioned the sentry. "As a ranger, I thought a man like you would be tracking down an outlaw."

"He's a frisky little cat," said Ranger Bob. "He was always jumping after mosquitoes and all sorts of bugs. And, like all cats, he was fascinated by birds. You ever see him?"

"Light gray and white?" noted the sentry. "Pretty yellow-green eyes."

"Yes, sir, that's Skeeter all right," said Ranger Bob. "Where is he?"

"He's gone," replied the sentry.

"Gone?" said Ranger Bob with a worried look. "You see, the cat reminded me of another cat I had when I was little. And when I was on long patrols thinking about him, I was reminded of my childhood home. It was very comforting. But now that he's passed on...."

"Oh, no, he's fine," interrupted the sentry.

Ranger Bob beamed with joy.

"Captain Parker's daughter visited here about a month ago and fell in love with the cat," said the sentry. "She took him back with her to her ranch near Houston. I guess the cat's got the run of the Parker Ranch by now."

Ranger Bob stood there for a moment and said nothing.

"You expected the cat to be here, I reckon?" asked the sentry.

Ranger Bob nodded his head.

"I guess she has a real home now, and that's a good thing," said Ranger Bob. "But I sure do miss that cat. I could never keep him, of course, since I was always riding here and there."

"All the best to you, sir," said the sentry.

"Thank you," replied Ranger Bob as he mounted his horse.

"Where's your next assignment?" asked the sentry.

"Houston," answered Ranger Bob with a smile. "But first I'm going to look up a friend nearby at the Parker Ranch – a frisky, little friend who used to live here at the Alamo."

Tooz
1866

MARCH 6, 1866 FELL ON A TUESDAY. It was the thirtieth anniversary of the Battle of the Alamo, and the U.S. Army soldiers stationed at the old mission paid their respects to the fallen heroes during a special morning ceremony.

The first Tuesday of each month was important to the soldiers because it was the day that mail usually arrived. The soldiers appreciated the letters they received from their families back home. The handwritten letters were the only way that the soldiers could communicate with their loved ones and friends. When the mail wagon entered the Alamo grounds, Sergeant Ballentine shouted: "Mail call! Line up for mail call!"

Sergeant Ballentine stood six-feet tall. He was a rugged veteran who had joined the service in 1846 when the Mexican War began. He took his job very seriously and never seemed to smile. But that was about to change.

The men lined up next to the wagon and waited for the mail bag to be pulled from underneath the canvas cover. As they waited, the cover seemed to move. Then some of the soldiers started to laugh when they saw a scrawny white cat with long whiskers peek out from under the canvas.

"Quiet in the ranks!" commanded the sergeant, who didn't notice the cat.

The soldiers tried to hide their amusement, but they could not keep from smiling. The cat walked along the side of the wagon nearest the sergeant.

Sergeant Ballentine turned around and faced the cat which seemed to be looking directly at him. The cat yawned and lifted its right paw across its long, curved whiskers. The sergeant slowly began to smile. The soldiers couldn't believe their eyes: Sergeant Ballentine smiled!

The wagon driver looked back and saw the cat as it crawled back under the canvas.

"Well now, is this cat with the United States Post Office?" joked Sergeant Ballentine.

The soldiers started to laugh.

"Of course not, he's just a cat," said the wagon driver. "I didn't even know he was back there or how he got there. In any event, he can't stay in the postal wagon. It's against regulations."

"Then we've got to do something, sergeant," said one of the soldiers

"But what?" asked the bugler.

"We should make him our mascot," said another soldier.

"But we can't have a mascot," replied the bugler. "I think it's against Army regulations."

Sergeant Ballentine thought for a moment.

"A recruit!" stated the sergeant. "We'll accept him as a recruit in the United States Army. And that will be according to regulations."

The soldiers cheered.

Sergeant Ballentine understood that the cat reminded some of the men of their pets and families at home. And the soldiers appreciated the cute little fellow.

"Corporal Smith," commanded the sergeant, "carry that cat to the kitchen and feed him."

After the soldiers finished reading their letters from home, several visited the cat which had fallen asleep outside of the kitchen.

"Handsome little guy," said one of the soldiers.

"He certainly impressed the sergeant," said one of the cooks. "The sergeant seems like a new man."

"And I'm glad the sergeant gave him a home," said Corporal Smith.

"He needs a name," said another soldier.

"But what shall we name him?" asked one of the cooks.

"He's got a certain quality about him," said the bugler. "So it's got to be a special name,"

"Well, he arrived by mail," said Corporal Smith. "That doesn't happen every day."

"And he also arrived in a wagon," said a soldier.

"I think I've got an idea," said the cook. "He arrived on a Tuesday. How about we call him Tooz, short for Tuesday?"

"I like that," said Corporal Smith. "It's certainly a different name." The other soldiers smiled in agreement.

"Me too," said Sergeant Ballentine. "Tooz it is!"

Tooz remained at the Alamo for several years. The soldiers were amused by his actions especially when he hunted lizards and mice.

One day, a mouse sat outside one of the soldier's canvas tents eating a small biscuit crumb. Inside, the soldier was fast asleep. Quietly, Tooz approached the mouse very slowly. Several soldiers noticed that Tooz was on the hunt. The cat carefully took one step at a time until he was within two feet of the mouse. In the blink of an eye, Tooz leaped on the mouse and tossed him in the air. The mouse landed on the sleeping soldier's leg and Tooz pounced on the mouse.

"Hey!" cried the soldier as he awoke.

The other soldiers laughed as Tooz grasped the mouse in his mouth and ran outside the tent.

"I haven't seen a mouse around the kitchen area since Tooz arrived," said one of the cooks. "He's a real tiger."

Although Tooz was friendly with all the soldiers, he spent most of his time near Sergeant Ballentine. They enjoyed each other's company.

Like all cats, Tooz spent most of his time sleeping. Sleep was important because it allowed the cat to gain energy for hunting. His favorite sleeping spot was on a gray folded army blanket under Sergeant Ballentine's desk. When the sergeant copied his officers' orders, the scratching sound of the ink pen awakened Tooz. The cat was fascinated by the sound of the pen. Tooz would immediately jump on the desk and watch Sergeant Ballentine.

One evening, the sergeant was copying the second page of special orders when Tooz suddenly jumped upon the desk and nearly knocked over the ink well.

"Meow!"

"Now then, Private Tooz, you remove yourself from this desk," grinned Sergeant Ballentine. "I've got official business to write."

Tooz didn't move.

The sergeant gently lifted the cat and placed him on the ground.

"Scat, now," said Sergeant Ballentine. "You spend too much time with me. Go fetch a mouse or something. The captain needs these orders copied right away. So Scat!"

Tooz scurried out of the room.

About a half hour later, Sergeant Ballentine finished copying the orders. But he had one more document to write: his resignation letter. The sergeant was not going to reenlist in the U.S. Army. He was retiring from active duty after twenty years of service. He had fought in several battles during the Mexican War and received a musket ball wound in his left arm. Sergeant Ballentine had faithfully served his country. As he finished the letter, he turned around in his chair and noticed Tooz sitting in the doorway. His right paw rested on a dead mouse.

The sergeant smiled from ear to ear.

"You are some cat, Tooz," exclaimed Sergeant Ballentine. "When you want to sleep, you sleep. And when I tell you to fetch a mouse, you catch one!"

The next day, Sergeant Ballentine informed the soldiers that he was leaving the service in a month.

"I'm going to be a civilian again, men," he said. "I'll be settling in Austin, and I wish you all well."

On his last day of service, Sergeant Ballentine waited for the stagecoach to arrive.

"Stagecoach approaching," yelled the sentry.

Corporal Smith and the enlisted men formed ranks. They had spent hours dusting off their uniforms and shining their boots. They wanted to look their best on Sergeant Ballentine's last day. After a brief ceremony in which the commanding officer thanked him for his dedicated years of service, the soldiers presented Sergeant Ballentine with a wooden box. The box had a handle and holes placed along its ends.

"What's all this about?" asked the sergeant.

"A parting gift for you, sergeant," said Corporal Smith.

"I guess I can find a useful purpose for this," said Sergeant Ballentine. "I thank you all."

The soldiers cheered as the sergeant tipped his hat at the men.

"But I've got one final order for all of you," he commanded. "Take good care of Tooz."

"Yes, sergeant," replied Corporal Smith. "Of course, sergeant. He'll have the best possible care."

The soldiers smiled as he lifted the box on the coach.

Sergeant Ballentine didn't realize that the gift wasn't the box. The gift was inside the box.

From inside the box came a familiar sound: "Meow!"

The sergeant knew who was inside.

Tooz and Sergeant Ballentine were going to their new home.

Wuckie
1886

FIFTY YEARS AFTER THE FAMOUS BATTLE of the Alamo, few visitors were able to recognize the famous mission fortress. The Long Barrack building was covered with a large wooden storefront built by the Hugo and Schmeltzer Company, which sold everything from clothes to furniture. And the nearby Alamo Church was used as a warehouse. It just didn't look proper to those who remembered the Alamo.

San Antonio was growing. It was very different from the town that was home to several hundred citizens in the 1830s. Thanks to the Galveston, Harrisburg and San Antonio Railroad, which linked the city to the rest of the country, thousands of people flocked to San Antonio in the 1880s. New businesses were starting up everywhere. Horse-drawn wagons carried produce from the farms to the town markets. San Antonio was a busy place especially around Alamo Plaza.

Deborah was a bookkeeper who worked in the Hugo and Schmeltzer Company store. She knew about the Alamo because her grandfather had fought in the Texas Revolution and had told her stories about the bravery of the Alamo heroes.

She worked in a small room near the open courtyard. Each afternoon during her lunch break, she walked the grounds of the Alamo and remembered some of the names of the Alamo defenders that her grandfather had mentioned to her when she was a little girl: Travis, Crockett, Bowie, Esparza,

Bonham, Losoya and Dickinson.

One day on one of her walks, a friend, Helene, approached her carrying a basket.

"Deborah, you have to help me," said Helene.

"How?" asked Deborah.

"Old man Russel showed up at our farm and gave us this cat," said Helene, as she lifted the lid of the basket. "He said he couldn't take care of her anymore. I took the cat but my cousin moved in with us and brought his dogs. They kept scaring the cat. Can you help me and take care of her?"

"I'd like to help but I can't keep the cat in the boarding house where I live," said Deborah. "The owner won't allow it."

"I know that, but perhaps you can take care of it here for a while," said Helene. "There's plenty of room in the courtyard and no one comes out here much."

"Here, at work?" questioned Deborah. "I have enough work to do without taking care of a cat. And if my supervisor finds out, I could lose my job."

The dark gray cat's head popped up through the basket lid and yawned. Deborah scratched his head and the cat started to purr. The cat was all gray, but its eyes were green.

"He likes you," said Helene. "The old man called him Wuckie."

"Wuckie?" replied Deborah.

"I think it's a Comanche name," said Helene.

"Comanche?" exclaimed Deborah. "My father told me that they were the fiercest warriors in all of Texas."

"Please?" pleaded Helene. "I don't know what else to do with Wuckie."

Deborah carefully considered her friend's request.

"All I can do is provide him with some milk during my lunch break," said Deborah. "That's all I can promise. And he's on his own, especially on Sunday when no one is here."

Helene smiled and thanked Deborah who placed the open basket near a cluster of bushes. Wuckie hesitated and then leaped out of the basket.

"You certainly have the longest legs I've ever seen on a cat," exclaimed Deborah. "I bet that no mouse is safe from you."

Every day for the next few weeks, Deborah placed a saucer of milk near the hidden basket by the side of the Alamo church. Wuckie would quickly emerge from his leaf-covered rest area and drink the milk. When he was finished, he would run away to play or find a place to sleep.

As an orphan who provided for a younger sister, Deborah worked over sixty hours a week. Deborah was concerned that her fellow employees would not want the cat around the workplace. Perhaps one of them would tell the supervisor. But when they met him, all the workers fell in love with Wuckie. They brought him scraps of food and soon Wuckie traveled all over the old Alamo grounds looking for a meal or someone to play with.

One day, Deborah was called in to the supervisor's office.

"I have been informed that you have brought a cat onto the premises," said the supervisor.

"I'm sorry, sir," said Deborah. "I don't want to lose my job."

"Fear not, young lady," he replied. "As long as you don't neglect your work and you take care of the cat on your time, it won't be a problem."

"Then why did you call me into your office, sir?" asked Deborah.

"Here, take this," said the supervisor as he handed Deborah a small bag of bacon. "My cat at home loves bacon. Wuckie will too."

Deborah smiled as she returned to her desk.

One day Deborah saw Wuckie climbing along the second floor railing of the storefront. Wuckie paused to look at the birds flying by.

"How did you get so far up there, little one?" she asked. "Be careful up there, Wuckie. Watch your step."

On another occasion, Wuckie was seen climbing atop the boxes stored in the Alamo Church.

"That cat certainly knows his way around here," said a warehouse worker to Deborah.

"He's an Alamo cat," she replied.

One afternoon, Deborah walked in the courtyard to retrieve the saucer but noticed that the milk wasn't touched. Wuckie was nowhere to be seen. She returned the next day with a saucer of fresh milk but once again the cat did not appear. Deborah was concerned. She asked the other workers if they had seen the cat but they said they had not.

Although her work place was closed on Sunday, Deborah traveled to the Alamo to look for the cat. She arrived early in the morning and searched the area for about an hour. Still, Wuckie could not be found. Deborah worried about his safety.

When Deborah arrived at work the next day, she was greeted by a fellow worker who told her that she had a visitor waiting for her at her desk. It was Wuckie!

"Where have you been?" asked Deborah as she picked up the cat and stroked its chin. "I was very worried about you." Wuckie started to purr.

Deborah carried the cat back to the bushes and gently placed it down. Wuckie looked up at Deborah but a butterfly soon got his attention. He crouched and stalked the butterfly for the next few minutes until he sprang upon it.

"You are quite the hunter, Wuckie," said Deborah. "You deserve some milk."

By the time she returned with the saucer of milk, Helene was standing in the courtyard.

"Hello, Helene," said Deborah. "As you can see, it's milk time for Wuckie."

"They're gone," said Helene.

"Who's gone?" asked Deborah as she placed the saucer on the ground.

"The dogs," answered Helene. "My cousin moved out and took his dogs with him. I can bring Wuckie home."

Deborah hesitated for a moment. She wanted to tell her friend that the Alamo was Wuckie's new home, but she realized that she had made her friend a promise. As soon as Wuckie finished the milk she lifted him and placed him in Helene's basket.

"You'll take good care of him, won't you?" asked Deborah.

"Of course," replied Helene.

"I'm going to miss that cat," admitted Deborah. "In fact, I'm going to miss him very much."

Helene realized that Deborah cared very much about Wuckie.

"I could bring Wuckie here for a visit," said. Helene. "And you can always visit him at my house."

Deborah was sad. She regarded Wuckie as more than just an animal. She treated the cat like a member of her small family but she realized that the cat would no longer be around.

"Are you all right?" asked Helene.

"Yes," said Deborah with a sigh. "Oh, Helene, I would very much like to visit Wuckie at your house."

Suddenly a "meow" sounded and the basket lid flew open. Wuckie jumped out and ran straight for the bushes.

Helene understood that Wuckie didn't want to leave the Alamo. She smiled at Deborah and grasped both of her hands.

"I think Wuckie wants this to be his home," said Helene.

"I think so, too," declared Deborah. "He's an Alamo cat now."

Red
1916

THE STATE OF TEXAS HAD PURCHASED the Long Barrack building in 1883, but the Alamo Church was in private hands. Gustav Schmeltzer of the Hugo and Schmeltzer Company offered to sell the Alamo for $75,000 in 1903. One potential buyer wanted to turn the Alamo into a hotel.

Adina de Zavala, president of the De Zavala Chapter of the Daughters of the Republic of Texas (DRT), an organization formed in 1891 to honor the memory of Texas pioneers, believed that the Alamo should be preserved as an important historical site, not as a hotel or a place of business. She sought donations to help buy the place where the Alamo heroes fought and died for Texas freedom in 1836. But she only managed to raise about a few thousand dollars.

Fortunately, Clara Driscoll, a new member of the Daughters of the Republic of Texas, came to the rescue. She generously provided over $65,000 to cover the purchase of the Alamo.

The Alamo was saved.

In 1905, Clara Driscoll gave the Alamo's land title to the state of Texas. The state, in turn, returned her money and gave the Daughters of the Republic of Texas the authority to act as the official custodians of the Alamo.

The Daughters of the Republic of Texas were now responsible for maintaining and protecting the centuries-old mission. The women wanted the place to look inviting to all who visited the Shrine of Texas Liberty.

In the spring of 1914, local workers were hired to landscape the property. On one sunny April day as new Red Woodbine bushes and an oak tree were being planted, a small bright orange and white-colored cat strolled onto the property. He climbed atop a wagon and watched the workers.

"Who are you, our supervisor?" grinned one of the workers.

"He's looking for a handout," said another.

One of the workers placed small piece of beef from a sandwich on the cart. The cat quickly ate the food.

"Slow down, Red," said another worker.

"I like that name," said the foreman. "His fur almost looks red in the sunlight."

From that day on, Red was part of the work crew which landscaped the Alamo grounds. No one knew where he spent the night, but each morning the cat appeared and the workers promptly fed him.

One worker was concerned that Red might become too dependant on the men for his food.

"You know, once we finish this part of the job we'll be gone," he said. "And then there will be no food for Red."

"Don't worry," said another worker. "Red must have done well before he ever saw us, and I suspect he'll be quite all right after we leave."

One afternoon, Red appeared as the workers sat down to eat their lunch.

"Here, Red," said the foreman. "I've got some beef for you."

But Red just sat and stared at the men.

"No appetite today, Red?" said a worker who sat near the cat.

Red leaned down and looked at a small snake that he had caught. He picked up the lifeless creature in his teeth and walked over to the foreman were he promptly dropped it.

"Meow!" cried Red.

The men all laughed.

"Well, how about that!" said the foreman. "The hunter has brought us some food." He reached down and gently scratched the cat's head. "We're not much for snakes, Red, but we appreciate your gift."

Red playfully flipped the snake around a few times and then carried it

back to the line of freshly planted bushes.

"I guess that after we're done working here, Red will be able to fend for himself after all," said one of the workers.

"If he can catch snakes, I don't think he'll have a problem catching other critters," said the foreman.

The next day, Red was waiting for the workers in the newly planted oak tree. He sat on the small tree's longest branch and looked at them.

"Be careful, Red," warned one of the workers. "Don't fall."

Red's attention quickly shifted to a sparrow flying over the courtyard. His whiskers started to twitch but he remained almost motionless as the bird landed on the top of the Alamo Church. Then the bird swooped down and landed on a branch near Red.

The men paused in their work to see what was going to happen next.

Red's body started to quiver and his ears turned to the sound of the bird. In a moment, Red leaped at the sparrow but the bird narrowly escaped his outstretched claws. Red grasped the branch in desperation with his front paws.

"Hang on, Red," shouted the foreman.

Red tried to lift himself up but started to lose his grip. The men dropped their shovels and ran towards him, but before they could reach him he slipped. Fortunately, as he fell, Red twisted his body and managed to land on his four legs. He immediately started to groom himself as if the dangerous moment never had happened.

"Red, you're a lucky cat, that's for sure," said the foreman. "Had this been an older oak, a taller tree, you could have hurt yourself."

Red looked up at the foreman.

"Meow!"

"That's right," said the foreman. "You are one lucky cat."

Red returned the next day and climbed the tree. But one worker would always stay close by just in case the cat tried something risky.

On the last day of the landscaping project, the workers brought special treats for Red. Some brought tiny strips of beef; others brought bits of pork. Red enjoyed the food that the men had brought him.

Then all the workers took turns petting Red before they left. The cat purred with every touch. The men enjoyed Red's companionship while on the job and they believed that the cat appreciated them as well.

The men placed their tools on the horse-drawn wagon and then they climbed aboard. As the wagon pulled away, the men looked back at the Alamo but at first they couldn't see Red.

"Hey, look!" said one of the workers. "He's up in the tree."

"Where?" said another worker.

"At the end of the long branch," said the foreman.

"Yeah, there he is," said another worker. "It's as if he wanted us to see him one more time."

The foreman nodded his head in agreement.

"I think he'll be fine," said the foreman. "He's a tough little guy."

Months later, the foreman returned to the Alamo. He walked in the courtyard and noticed that the bushes and oak tree had grown. His was proud that he and the other men helped make the grounds of the Alamo look more attractive. He smiled as he remembered how Red used to climb the oak tree.

A sparrow swooped down from the top of the Alamo Church and landed on one of the oak tree's branches.

For a moment, the foreman thought he heard a "meow." "Could it be Red?" he thought.

He looked around but saw nothing.

Red was gone.

"I'll miss you, Red," whispered the foreman as he walked away. "You'll always be our Alamo cat."

Tuxedo
1936

THE YEAR 1936 WAS THE CENTENNIAL of the Texas Revolution and the Daughters of the Republic of Texas were going to celebrate the 100th anniversary of the Battle of the Alamo in grand style. It would be a special year to remember the Alamo.

Ceremonies honoring the Alamo heroes were planned, and President Franklin D. Roosevelt scheduled a visit to the Shrine of Texas Liberty. Various events were held throughout the year, but one function had a special guest – and it wasn't the President of the United States. In fact, it was an uninvited guest.

A formal dinner was arranged at the historic seventy-seven year old Menger Hotel which was located across the street from the Alamo. It was held on a splendid March evening. Outside, the guests arrived. The ladies wore fine long dresses with white gloves and the men wore tuxedos.

As the kitchen staff prepared the meal of fine cuts of beef and vegetables, the servers put finishing touches on the dining room. Flowers were carefully placed in vases on each table. Portraits of David Crockett, William Travis, Sam Houston, Juan Seguín and other Texas heroes were placed on the walls. Everything was in place. It was almost time for the first guests to enter the room.

All of a sudden, a slinky black and white cat confidently walked in the room as if she had an invitation.

"How did you get in here?" asked Millie, one of the servers. "I've got to get you out of here."

"Meow" said the cat as she continued her promenade.

"Look at her coloring," said another server. "It's like she's wearing a tuxedo."

The cat's body was primarily black except for her white paws. White fur covered her face but a black patch covered one eye and her nose. And a small patch of black fur, like a tiny bow tie, was located under her chin. Her shiny coat seemed to sparkle whenever she walked under the chandelier lighting.

"Maybe she thinks she belongs here," said a man who was carrying a stack of chairs. "She certainly looks like she's dressed for the occasion."

Everyone laughed.

The cat meowed again but it sounded more like a loud purr.

"She sounds like she belongs here, too!" said the man.

"I've never heard a cat meow like that before," said one of the servers. "It's as if she was trying to talk to us."

"She's just showing off," remarked the man.

Millie picked up the cat.

"Now look here, Miss Tuxedo, you may look the part but you don't have an invitation for this dinner," said Millie as she walked towards the delivery entrance. "I'm sorry, but I'm going to carry you out back."

Millie placed the cat at the side entrance to the hotel.

"Go on now," said Millie.

Tuxedo looked up at Millie and then scampered across Crockett Street before disappearing behind the bushes near the Alamo Church.

A day after the event, Millie was walking past the Alamo towards the Menger Hotel when she heard a unique "meow." She turned around and saw Tuxedo who meowed again.

"Well, good morning, Tuxedo," said Millie. "I thought that sounded like you." Tuxedo ran back into the bushes and Millie continued her walk to work. At the hotel, Millie told some of the other workers that she had seen Tuxedo at the Alamo.

"Tuxedo, the Alamo cat, eh?" said one of the workers. "I've heard that a lot of cats have lived at the Alamo since the big battle back in 1836."

"I suppose so," answered Millie. "I've only seen her here and at the Alamo."

At the end of the work day, Millie slowly walked past the Alamo in an attempt to meet the cat again. Tuxedo didn't disappoint. She sounded a loud meow from her position on the courtyard oak tree. Millie walked toward the tree and saw Tuxedo sitting proudly on a branch.

"Good evening, Tuxedo," greeted Millie. "We meet again."

The cat walked toward the tree's trunk and climbed down. Millie welcomed her by scratching her back. Tuxedo immediately collapsed to the ground and started twisting from side to side. And she started to purr.

"You sure do look content," smiled Millie as she gently petted the cat. "I hope I see you tomorrow, Tuxedo."

Tuxedo delivered one of her special-sounding meows as she continued to roll back and forth on the ground. Millie started to laugh as the dirt began to fly around Tuxedo's twisting body. Finally, Tuxedo stopped her lively movements and began grooming herself.

When Millie returned to work, she explained to her co-workers how Tuxedo twisted and rolled on the ground when she was happy.

"I've got to see that," said one of the workers. "I thought only dogs did that kind of rolling around on the ground."

"I want to see that, too!" replied another worker.

Tuxedo didn't appear at the hotel nor was she seen at the Alamo the next day. A week passed but no one saw Tuxedo anywhere. Every day, Millie walked very slowly past the Alamo in the hope that she would see Tuxedo.

Finally, after three weeks, Tuxedo showed up at the Menger Hotel's delivery entrance. She announced herself with a loud meow.

One of the workers saw the cat and went inside to alert everyone. Within minutes, Millie arrived and began scratching Tuxedo's back. "Where have you been?" asked Millie. "We missed you."

As a dozen workers watched, the cat began twisting back and forth on her back. They smiled, enjoying her unique behavior.

"Tuxedo, you certainly made another memorable visit," said Millie as she lifted the cat into her arms. "But we have to leave now because we have jobs to do. We have to wash all of the sheets and pillowcases. You be good until I see you again."

Millie lowered the cat to the delivery entrance landing and Tuxedo promptly ran towards the Alamo grounds. They all looked as she crossed the street and scurried among the flowers.

"What is it about that cat?" asked one of the workers. "She's not like other cats."

"Tuxedo is different from other cats I've known," said Millie. "She behaves differently and sounds different. There's something special about her, but I just don't know what it is."

Millie made it a point to see Tuxedo the next day and nearly every day after that. She brought her small pieces of meat each evening and placed them near the bushes. Tuxedo was grateful for the food, and Millie was pleased to provide the tidbits.

"Don't worry, Tuxedo, I'll always be close by to watch out for you," said Millie. "After all, we're friends. And I promise I'll always be your friend."

In the winter time, Tuxedo would sit under the automobiles that pulled into the parking lot next to the Alamo. She appreciated the warmth from the cars' engines. Once the engines cooled off, she returned to a corner in the Long Barrack building where she felt safe.

Tuxedo was fascinated by a rare snowfall during the winter of 1938. She had never seen snowflakes before. Even Millie hadn't seen much snow in San Antonio. Tuxedo jumped up and bit the snowflakes as they fell. She was having a grand time.

"I bet you think they're little white moths or something," laughed Millie as Tuxedo sprang up and swallowed another snowflake. "I've got to get back to work. I'll see you when I end my day."

Tuxedo continued to play in the snow.

After the snow flurries stopped, Tuxedo ran to her new favorite spot in the corner of the Long Barrack building. She groomed herself and nestled down for a long nap.

Once her work day was over, Millie stopped by to see Tuxedo. The cat was curled up in a ball with her paws over her face. Tuxedo felt safe and secure at the Alamo like earlier cats.

"Sleep well, Miss Tuxedo," said Millie as she looked down at the black and white ball of fur. "Sleep well."

While she worked at the hotel, Millie and Tuxedo exchanged morning and evening greetings for many years. They both enjoyed each other's company. Even after Millie left her job and got married in 1943, she would regularly visit the Alamo to see Tuxedo.

Millie kept her word to Tuxedo.

They were friends.

Forever.

Ruby
1986

DURING THE SUMMER OF 1981, ANOTHER CAT became part of the Alamo story.

While on patrol one hot August night, Alamo Ranger Chuck heard a high-pitched sound. He paused and looked around.

"Meow" came a cry from above.

He looked at a tree and saw a calico kitten crying from one of its branches.

"How did you get up there?" asked the ranger.

The kitten meowed again.

The cat was too high in the tree for the ranger to reach it, so he coaxed it down with a cup of milk. The kitten carefully climbed down the tree and sat near the cup. The ranger placed a few drops of milk on the cat's mouth and placed the animal closer to the cup. The kitten drank all of the milk.

"That's it for you," said the ranger with grin. "You go on now. This isn't your home."

Ranger Chuck walked away and continued making his rounds but he noticed that the kitten was close behind.

"Hey, I'm not your mother," stated the ranger with a laugh. "And I have a job to do. So be on your way."

The ranger continued to walk the Alamo grounds. He made sure all of the buildings were locked and that no one had trespassed. Every now and then he looked around to see if the kitten was following him but it was nowhere to be seen. But when he returned to his office the kitten was waiting for him.

"How did you manage to get in here?" smiled the ranger. "I'll never leave that door open again."

The kitten let out a big meow.

"I know what you want: food!" said the ranger. He opened his chicken sandwich and gave the kitten a few small pieces. The kitten finished the generous offering and looked up at the ranger.

"Look at your eyes," he said. "They're so big and green."

He carefully lifted the kitten and carried it to the edge of the Alamo grounds.

"I'm sorry but you can't stay here," said the ranger. "I'm going off duty now, and I guess I won't see you again."

Ranger Chuck left the Alamo but returned to work the next evening. Within minutes of his first walk near the rear of the Alamo Church he heard a familiar meow.

"You're back again, eh, Ruby?" said the ranger who promptly shared a piece of his sandwich with the cat. "Yes, Ruby! I like the sound of the name, like the tiny precious gemstone."

The young cat returned every night. During the day, other rangers and Alamo staff members had seen the cat as it climbed trees and leaped from branch to branch. Whenever they could, the rangers kept a watchful eye out for her during the day.

Soon, everyone fell in love with the cute little cat. And everyone wanted the Alamo to be its home. The Daughters of the Republic of Texas allowed Ruby to be a part of the Alamo once it got proper vaccinations from a veterinarian.

"Ruby needed those shots to keep her as healthy as possible," said Ranger Will.

Ruby quickly became an active part of the Alamo family. She leaped among the bushes, played with butterflies, chased squirrels and stalked unsuspecting tourists. Ruby defended her home like a true Alamo defender.

She became bigger, stronger and more playful around the Alamo staff. Everyone admired her gleaming fur and her lush whiskers.

Early the next year, Ruby became a mother. Everyone was excited. On February 2, 1982, Ruby gave birth to six kittens: four males and two females. Each kitten was given a name – like Bowie Crockett – which was composed of the combined names of various Alamo heroes. Ruby was given a last name: Le Gato. *Gato* is Spanish for cat. And the Daughters of the Republic issued a birth announcement. It was a special event at the Alamo.

Ruby and her kittens became instant celebrities. The local newspapers and TV crews reported on the Alamo births. Wisely, Ruby was taken to a veterinarian who successfully spayed her. The operation prevented Ruby from having more kittens.

As the weeks passed, the kittens grew rapidly and began to play all over the Long Barrack building. Ranger Chuck knew that he and the other Alamo staff members could not care for seven cats. He wondered if anyone would be willing to adopt Ruby's kittens.

"I'd like to adopt one of them," said Kim, who worked in the Gift Museum.

"I'll take the two females," noted Marie, one of the DRT Alamo Library staff members.

"My wife said that she would like one of them," replied one of the rangers.

Within days, all of the kittens were claimed.

Ruby enjoyed chasing the birds that landed near the *acequia,* a ditch that held water. One day she jumped after a bird and landed in the *acequia*. Since the ditch's walls were tall and straight Ruby found it difficult to climb out. One evening, Ruby fell in but, fortunately, Ranger Mike saw her and promptly pulled her out. She shook the water from her fur and ran into the flower bed near the large oak tree.

"You're lucky I was nearby, Ruby," said the ranger. "You've got to be more careful when you go after those birds."

On March 6, 1986, people from all over the world came to San Antonio to honor the Alamo heroes who had died 150 years earlier. Special ceremonies were held in front of the Alamo Church at dawn. Prayers were said for the fallen heroes and a musket volley was fired in their honor.

Later, when it opened, the Alamo greeted thousands of visitors. Ruby knew that the best way to stay away from the many human feet was to relax on one of the oak tree's large limbs or nap in the DRT Library where she enjoyed sitting on the display cases.

One night weeks later, Ranger Chuck heard some unusual sounds in the Alamo courtyard. He quickly walked over and saw Ruby staring down a large raccoon near the *acequia*. The ranger knew that the raccoon had an advantage in size and strength over Ruby, especially if they both ended up in the water. Ruby's back arched as she prepared to jump at the animal, but the ranger quickly picked Ruby up and the pair chased the raccoon from the Alamo grounds.

"Nice going, Ruby!" said the ranger as he gently placed her on the ground. "Wait until I tell everyone about your bravery."

The Alamo Rangers were the first to hear about Ruby's stand against the raccoon. Within minutes of the Alamo's opening, the entire staff knew about the cat's bravery. Everyone who saw Ruby congratulated her for defending the Alamo. Ruby's effort to protect the Shrine of Texas Liberty from four-legged creatures was properly acknowledged when San Antonio College awarded her a Basic Security Officer Training Certificate.

"Ruby, you are now an official security guard here at the Alamo," said Ranger Chuck. "I'm proud of you!"

Ruby continued to enjoy her life at the Alamo. She was loved by all who knew her. Visitors to Texas' most famous historical site were amused by her whether she was playing in the courtyard or napping on a display case.

One evening, Ranger Chuck arrived at the Alamo for his night shift. He entered the Alamo Rangers' office where two rangers starred at him. Chuck sensed that something was wrong.

"What's the problem?" asked Chuck. "Why the sad faces?"

The two rangers looked at each other but they were speechless. They could not explain to Chuck why they looked so sorrowful.

"Well?" questioned Chuck.

"It's Ruby," said one of the rangers finally.

"What about her?" asked Chuck.

"She's gone," whispered the other. "We found her in the *acequia.* We don't know how it happened. Maybe it was the raccoon. But we just don't know."

Ranger Chuck couldn't speak. He lifted his hands to his face and wiped the tears from his eyes.

It was a sad day at the Alamo.

Ruby was gone but she would always be remembered.

Ruby was so loved by the Daughters of the Republic of Texas, the Alamo Rangers and others who worked at the Alamo, that a bronze plaque was placed at her burial site in the courtyard.

RUBY
The Alamo Cat
1981-1986

Late at night when Ranger Chuck patrolled the grounds he would always stop and pay his respects to Ruby at her grave site. He removed his hat and reached for the bronze marker. He tapped it a few times.

"We miss you, Ruby," he said. "Thanks for all the joy you brought us."

He looked up into the clear star-filled sky and wondered what Ruby had thought of all the tiny dots of light. Suddenly a shooting star appeared in distant western sky above the Alamo Church.

"Ruby?" said Ranger Chuck.

And then he smiled.

C.C.
2011

THE MOST RECENT ADDITION TO THE LONG LINE of Alamo cats is C.C., a beautiful white feline with splashes of black fur and golden amber eyes.

When she first appeared on Alamo grounds during the 1996-97 winter she had no name, but the attractive young cat quickly established her identity as the queen of the territory.

"She walked around here as if she were royalty," said one Alamo worker. "It was as if this were her kingdom. And trespassers, whether they were human or other animals, were not welcome when she was walking around the Alamo."

At first, it appeared that the cat was not that friendly.

"When she first arrived at the Alamo she was a feral cat, as wild as wild could be," said Pattie, an Alamo office worker. "You could not even look at her without her hissing at you. When I first made contact with her I was shocked because of her angry behavior."

The cat continued to hiss when people approached her. But there was a reason for her guarded behavior: she was getting ready to become a mother. She soon gave birth to a litter of tiny kittens but, sadly, none of them survived.

In May of 1997, she gave birth to another litter. This time, all the kittens were healthy. Everyone at the Alamo was happy.

"They all look like little balls of fur," said one Alamo worker. "They're so cute. I'm going to adopt one."

"Me, too," said a member of the landscaping team.

"I'll take one home, too," exclaimed a lady from the Gift Museum.

Eventually, all of the kittens were claimed by Alamo employees.

But the cat did not approve of the adoptions.

"She was a very protective mother," said Pattie. "When her kittens were old enough to eat on their own we tried to catch the babies and distribute them to all those who adopted them. Jerry, one of the maintenance guys, picked up one of the kittens and it started screaming for dear life. The mother came running from behind the bushes and chased Jerry, hissing and clawing all the way! We eventually rounded up all the kittens, but it wasn't easy."

The cat looked for her babies for several days.

"She cried and searched for them," said Pattie. "One day, she finally realized that they were not coming back. But we had to make sure that all of her kittens would be properly taken care of."

Everyone agreed that the cat should not give birth to more kittens. It would be more difficult to find proper homes for future offspring. And there were already too many feral cats roaming the streets. A decision was made to spay the cat.

A member of the Daughters of the Republic of Texas offered to pay for her care at a veterinarian's office. Pattie and another Alamo employee, Virginia, volunteered to transport the cat to the veterinarian for the surgical procedure.

The surgery was scheduled for August 18, 1997, one day after David Crockett's 211th birthday.

"On the way to the doctor's office, we realized that she had to have a name," said Pattie. "We didn't have much time to select a name. We wondered if we should name her after an Alamo defender. But Virginia and I came up with Clara Carmack or C.C. for short."

C.C. represents the names of two important Alamo ladies: Clara Driscoll and Mary Carmack. Clara Driscoll, of course, provided her own money to purchase the Alamo Church in 1905; Mary Carmack served as the Daughters of the Republic's Alamo Committee Chairwoman in the 1990s.

"We brought her into the veterinarian's office, but we were concerned about her hissing and scratching at us," said Pattie. "The doctor said that he would take good care of her and the procedure wouldn't take that long. He assured us that C.C. would be all right."

The doctor and his assistant carried C.C. from the waiting room to the operating room. Pattie and Virginia had worried looks as they waved good-bye to C.C. Then they returned to the Alamo and waited.

Later in the day, Pattie received a phone call from the veterinarian's office.

"Hello, Pattie," said the doctor.

"How is C.C.?" asked Pattie.

"She is fine," replied the doctor. "Everything went well. You can pick her up in the evening."

"That's wonderful!" said Pattie. "I can't wait to see her again."

Pattie told Virginia the good news. Soon everyone at the Alamo learned that the operation was a success.

Upon her return to the Alamo C.C. slowly warmed up to the Alamo staff.

"I had tried to get close to C.C., but at first she would have nothing to do with me," said Pattie. "Then one day, everything changed. I attempted to approach her once again but she turned and went through a small opening by one of our courtyard walls. I reached my arm through the opening and that's when it happened. C.C. swiped at my hand, not with her claws, but with her soft paw. I nearly melted at her soft touch. From then on we were close friends."

But C.C. was still ferocious when she crossed paths with other animals who ventured onto the Alamo grounds.

"Birds, insects, mice, squirrels and other cats had better watch out when they come to the Alamo and C.C. is on guard," said one of the Alamo Rangers. "She's a beautiful-looking cat but don't be fooled by her appearance. C.C. is tough. She's all Texan, a true Alamo defender."

One day a stray cat waltzed through the rear entrance to the Alamo grounds and was quickly challenged by C.C. Both cats raised their backs and started to hiss at one another. They stared at each other for quite some time as their tails whipped back and forth. Then C.C. made a meow that sounded more like a growl, and the other cat ran away. She watched proudly as the other cat disappeared beyond the parking area near the Alamo Rangers headquarters. Then C.C. promptly rolled on the ground and started to purr.

"It looked like a victory dance," said one of the Alamo Rangers. "It was very funny."

A moment later, a bird landed about twenty feet away from her. C.C. quickly got to her feet and darted after the winged intruder. The bird escaped her claws as it flew for the safety of the Alamo Church roof. However, later that night, a mouse wasn't as lucky.

Sometimes, C.C. will immediately bond with someone.

"In 2003, I came in for a job interview and waited on a bench outside of the Gift Museum," said Tawnny. "While I was there I noticed a cat staring at me. I said, 'Hi, Kitty,' and she walked up to me and jumped in my lap. I guess she was welcoming me to my new job."

But Tawnny soon learned that C.C. was demanding.

"C.C. would come into the office where I worked and if I did not move out of my chair for her she would sit in front of my computer screen until I moved. She wanted my chair, and I was not going to get any work done on the computer until I gave her the chair. But we have a very good relationship."

Although C.C. is seen in many places at the Alamo, it's sometimes difficult to locate her.

"C.C. doesn't have an exact schedule at the Alamo," said Leslie, the library director. "She is seen just about everywhere and then she disappears from my sight for days at a time. That's just the way C.C. behaves. As an Alamo cat, she comes in and out of wherever she wants to and when she wants to. Some mornings when I arrive she'll see me and follow me to the door. And then she'll follow me right in."

On other days C.C. might be found exploring the second floor office of the Alamo Curator or she may be seen looking for butterflies and other insects near Alamo Hall.

"Before the Alamo opens, I usually see her sunning herself on the flagstone between the Alamo Church and the Gift Museum," said Bruce, the Alamo curator. "It's the perfect spot for people to come by and pet her. She will allow visitors to pet her but it's her choice. When she has had enough attention she retreats downstairs to the Gift Museum or to the support area which is closed to the public."

One winter afternoon, C.C. did something unique when she visited Bruce's office.

"She used to come up to my office and spend part of the day curled up on my desk or my lap," he said. "But one day she jumped on my shoulder and draped herself around my neck like a scarf!"

C.C. also responds to bi-lingual commands.

"It doesn't matter whether someone calls her for food in English or Spanish," said Pattie. "She's that smart."

Despite her gentle appearance, C.C. is a strong and agile cat.

"All she needs is one leap and she's on top of the hood or trunk of a car," said Juan, one of the Alamo Rangers. "Then she'll walk in a circle, stop and curl up. In a few minutes she's fast asleep."

"She loves to jump on top of the bookcases," said Rusty, who works in the DRT Alamo Library. "One of the book cases is 51-inches high. That's a jump of over four feet! Of course, once she's up there it's time for a nap."

"And when she's napping, C.C. does not want to be disturbed," said Chuck, a reference librarian.

C.C. enjoys the year-round quiet of the DRT Alamo Library.

"It's peaceful in here," said Caitlin, a library archivist. "And she likes it here in the winter. Of course when it's cold outside the library is even more inviting. The maintenance people let her in and then she wanders in and out my office. She likes to jump up on my lap when I'm trying to type. And then, at other times, C.C. gets into tight corners where she feels even more safe and secure."

One day, Caitlin was outside and heard C.C. meow. She looked around but couldn't locate her.

"I heard this meowing," said Caitlin. "It sounded like C.C. was in trouble. I walked towards the sound of her cries near the vending machines. I worried that she may have managed to crawl inside one of the machines. As I stood in front of the vending machines, the meowing stopped. But as I looked up I saw her on the top of one of them. She just sat there and looked at me. I guess C.C. was wondering why I looked so concerned. Then I broke out in a very big grin and she gave me a meow."

Sometimes C.C. takes amusing risks.

One day C.C. entered the library and noticed a stack of cardboard mailing tubes. She liked high places so she promptly jumped on top of the stack. As C.C. walked across the tops of the tubes they wobbled underneath her.

"She was balancing herself on about twenty tubes," said Caitlin. "It was very cute, but I don't know how she maintained her balance. After she jumped off, the tubes toppled to the floor. C. C.'s an amazing and adorable cat."

Visitors to the Alamo adore C.C., too.

"She's such a beautiful cat," said a woman from California. "Her eyes are so gorgeous."

"There's something relaxing about seeing a cat at the Alamo, a place where brave men fought back in 1836," said another visitor from New Hampshire.

"I've got two cats being cared for back home while I'm here with my

parents," said a girl from Tennessee. "C.C. makes me miss them more."

One afternoon in the Long Barrack building courtyard, an Alamo guide was conducting a tour with a group of school children. The kids stood around him as he told the exciting story of the Alamo. Suddenly, C.C. appeared and strolled behind him. The children started to giggle. The Alamo guide knew immediately what had happened. He paused and smiled as C.C. walked by and disappeared into the bushes.

"It's happened before," said the guide. "Sometimes C.C. just wants to be part of the Alamo story."

As C. C.'s reputation grew, reporters from newspapers, magazines and television programs arrived at the Alamo. They were all fascinated by the cat that was charming the Alamo staff and visitors at the Shrine of Texas Liberty.

Her photo first appeared in the *San Antonio Express-News* in 2002. Other published stories followed. In 2007, the newspaper printed a two-page story about C.C. that included five photographs of her. The next year, the *Los Angeles Times* published a story about C.C.

"Clearly, C.C. was getting well known beyond San Antonio," said Mary Jo, the Alamo Gift Museum manager. "Alamo visitors would come to the gift shop and ask if any C.C. items were for sale."

Currently, the Alamo Gift Museum stocks an assortment of C.C. items. The cat's image is featured on T-shirts, socks, a plush toy, puzzles, post cards, magnets and key chains.

"We're constantly updating our supply of C.C. items," said Mary Jo. "Everybody who meets C.C. wants to have a keepsake to remember her by. After all, she's the Alamo's mascot. She's that special."

Animal Planet, the popular cable television channel, sent a video team to the Alamo to film C.C. in 2010. Once again, C.C. was the center of attention. The film crew treated her like a celebrity.

"And she's so spoiled by the staff," said Pattie. "Everyone pets her when she is lounging around."

When C. C.'s not being watched by the Alamo's staff and its many visitors, she loves to explore every nook and cranny of the Alamo grounds. She's always searching for new places to rest and sleep.

"C.C. likes to relax in the employee lounge and my office," said Sally, an education program coordinator.

One day, Mary Jo entered the Alamo mailroom and saw C.C. sitting on the floor.

"I turned away for a moment and when I looked back she was gone," said Mary Jo. "In an instant she had disappeared like a ghost. I wondered where she had gone so quickly. I looked around and before long saw a familiar tail sticking out from a box of packing material. C.C. had found yet another new place to take a nap."

C.C. has officially been recognized as an "Excellent Employee" of the Alamo. Staff members raised $100 to purchase a commemorative brick that features her name. The brick, along with one created for Ruby, another beloved Alamo cat, was placed in a special walkway section across the street from the Alamo in the Gallagher Building which serves as an office for the Daughters of the Republic of Texas and Alamo staff members.

"A brick like that is a special acknowledgment of service," said an Alamo employee. "And C.C. has done great service here as a first-rate guardian here at the Alamo."

Late one night, C.C. patrolled the Alamo grounds. She walked silently passed the Alamo Church and paused outside the Long Barrack building. A gray-striped cat appeared near the oak tree. Surprisingly, neither C.C. nor the other cat became upset or angry. The visitor walked up to C.C., sniffed her face and continued on.

A few weeks later, the gray-striped cat showed up behind the DRT Alamo Library where C.C. was relaxing. Once again, the two cats approached each other but a fight never developed. Instead, both cats started to purr.

"I wonder if C.C. finally found a friend who wasn't a human," said a maintenance worker. "It's wonderful that they get along."

C.C. gets along with the Alamo's educational program coordinators because she discovered it was a great place to get food.

"We keep a stock of dried food for her here," said Sally. "When she stops by our office, she can snack all she wants. After all, she's our C. C."

When C.C. roams the Alamo grounds she follows in the footsteps of other famous felines. Skeeter was befriended by a Texas Ranger in the 1840s. Tooz became the mascot of the U. S. Army in the late 1860s, and Wuckie was cared for by a bookkeeper in the 1880s. Red was a favorite of the Alamo landscapers back in 1914, and Tuxedo was the darling of the 1936 Texas Centennial. Ruby, of course, was cared for by the entire Alamo staff in the 1980s, and her final resting place is on the grounds of the Alamo.

Most of all, C.C. also walks on the ground made famous by the valiant men who gave their lives fighting for Texas' freedom at the Alamo. She helps bring attention to the Shrine of Texas Liberty and helps people "Remember the Alamo!" She's been a good will ambassador for the Daughters of the Republic of Texas for many years.

Like every beloved cat, C.C. brings joy and amusement to all who meet her, but unlike most cats, she also has a special role: C.C. can proudly take her place as an Alamo cat.

Remember the Alamo!

Meow!